COMPLETE
MIXING GUIDE

Containing a Full List
of Formulas for Making
All Standard Fancy
Drinks, Alphabetically
Arranged, Carefully
Compiled and Edited;
Also Recipes for
Attractive Desserts

Published by
J. W. WUPPERMANN
NEW YORK

ANGOSTURA HORSE'S NECK

== A ==
POPULAR
SUMMER
DRINK

Place square block of ice and the peel of one lemon in tall glass; add one bottle gingerale; put one loaf of sugar in teaspoon and saturate thoroughly with Angostura Bitters. Drop the sugar and Bitters gently on top of the ice and lemon peel so that the Bitters will percolate slowly through the drink.

IDENTIFICATION

———

MY NAME IS

....

MY ADDRESS IS

....

....

IN CASE OF ACCIDENT
OR SERIOUS ILLNESS PLEASE
NOTIFY

....

....

....

1

YEARLY CALENDAR, 1908

JANUARY

S	M	T	W	T	F	S
.	.	.	1	2	3	4
5	6	7	8	9	10	11
12	13	14	15	16	17	18
19	20	21	22	23	24	25
26	27	28	29	30	31	.

FEBRUARY

S	M	T	W	T	F	S
.	.	.	.	.	.	1
2	3	4	5	6	7	8
9	10	11	12	13	14	15
16	17	18	19	20	21	22
23	24	25	26	27	28	29

MARCH

S	M	T	W	T	F	S
1	2	3	4	5	6	7
8	9	10	11	12	13	14
15	16	17	18	19	20	21
22	23	24	25	26	27	28
29	30	31	.	.	.	.

APRIL

S	M	T	W	T	F	S
.	.	.	1	2	3	4
5	6	7	8	9	10	11
12	13	14	15	16	17	18
19	20	21	22	23	24	25
26	27	28	29	30	.	.

MAY

S	M	T	W	T	F	S
.	.	.	.	.	1	2
3	4	5	6	7	8	9
10	11	12	13	14	15	16
17	18	19	20	21	22	23
24	25	26	27	28	29	30
31	.	.	.	.	.	.

JUNE

S	M	T	W	T	F	S
.	1	2	3	4	5	6
7	8	9	10	11	12	13
14	15	16	17	18	19	20
21	22	23	24	25	26	27
28	29	30	.	.	.	.

JULY

S	M	T	W	T	F	S
.	.	.	1	2	3	4
5	6	7	8	9	10	11
12	13	14	15	16	17	18
19	20	21	22	23	24	25
26	27	28	29	30	31	.

AUGUST

S	M	T	W	T	F	S
.	.	.	.	.	.	1
2	3	4	5	6	7	8
9	10	11	12	13	14	15
16	17	18	19	20	21	22
23	24	25	26	27	28	29
30	31	.	.	.	.	.

SEPTEMBER

S	M	T	W	T	F	S
.	.	1	2	3	4	5
6	7	8	9	10	11	12
13	14	15	16	17	18	19
20	21	22	23	24	25	26
27	28	29	30	.	.	.

OCTOBER

S	M	T	W	T	F	S
.	.	.	.	1	2	3
4	5	6	7	8	9	10
11	12	13	14	15	16	17
18	19	20	21	22	23	24
25	26	27	28	29	30	31

NOVEMBER

S	M	T	W	T	F	S
1	2	3	4	5	6	7
8	9	10	11	12	13	14
15	16	17	18	19	20	21
22	23	24	25	26	27	28
29	30	.	.	.	.	.

DECEMBER

S	M	T	W	T	F	S
.	.	1	2	3	4	5
6	7	8	9	10	11	12
13	14	15	16	17	18	19
20	21	22	23	24	25	26
27	28	29	30	31	.	.

ANGOSTURA
BITTERS
Celebrated
Appetizer of
Exquisite Flavor

DR. SIEGERT'S
The Only Genuine
BEWARE OF
SUBSTITUTES
Originated 1824

23 AWARDS AT PRINCIPAL
INTERNATIONAL EXPOSITIONS

A useful remedy in all complaints
arising from Weakness and Slug-
gishness of the Digestive
Organs, Malaria, Colic,
Diarrhoea and Colds

*As a general tonic, a tablespoon before
meals and before retiring*

MANUFACTURED ONLY BY

Dr. J. G. B. Siegert & Sons
Purveyors to H. M. the German Emperor
and King of Prussia
Originated 1824

DON'T USE
Stale Bottled Cocktails

A FANCY DRINK, to be a success, must be freshly made, and its ingredients of superior quality. Especially is this true of the Bitters, the ingredient which gives the predominant flavor to every fancy drink. Men have commonly been known to walk many blocks to obtain a drink that suited their palates.

The best bartender in the world cannot mix a suitable drink if the Bitters are inferior. There is no combination that will spoil business quicker than a good bartender, good whiskey and poor Bitters.

Remember that when your dealer sends you a cheap substitute or imitation of

DR. SIEGERT'S
GENUINE IMPORTED
Angostura Bitters

It means that he is making a bigger profit on the substitute.

Any bitters called **ANGOSTURA** not made by the Siegerts is fraudulent

4

WHO GETS
The Best of This Game?

READ THIS:
IT WON'T TAKE A MINUTE

HAVE YOU ever been imposed upon by having some dealer send you **A Cheap Domestic Imitation of Dr.** Siegert's **Angostura Bitters Because He Made More Money on it?**

Domestic Substitutes of Dr. Siegert's **Imported Angostura Bitters** cost at wholesale about **Thirty Cents Per Bottle**, but the saloon proprietor pays as much as **Sixty-five Cents Per Bottle** for these spurious goods which have neither flavor nor strength.

One bottle DR. SIEGERT'S goes as far as THREE BOTTLES OF ANY IMITATION and costs only 10c. per bottle more.

Compare DR. SIEGERT'S with any other bitters you have ever used and judge for yourself.

SAVE MONEY by using the GENUINE IMPORTED ANGOSTURA exclusively.

THE BITTERS THAT
ORIGINATED THE COCKTAIL

If you stick to it, it will make money for you by winning trade from your short-sighted competitor.

ITS FLAVOR IS UNEQUALED

5

ANGOSTURA BITTERS

Originated 1824

THE BEST TONIC
AND APPETIZER

This drink, taken before meals, means increased appetite, good digestion, rich blood and healthy tissue.

Angostura Phosphate

Use a phosphate glass.

½ teaspoonful acid phosphate.

1 teaspoonful Dr. Siegert's Angostura Bitters. (THE ONLY GENUINE.)

2 tablespoonfuls lemon syrup, or juice of ½ lemon well sweetened.

Fill glass with carbonic water.

STANDARD
MIXED DRINKS

AND

OTHER FORMULAS

For Soda Fountain Drinks, see page 57

Attractive Desserts page 71

SPECIAL

WEST INDIAN SWIZZLE

(Use a shaker.) 1 teaspoonful of DR. SIEGERT'S ANGOSTURA BITTERS (the only genuine); $\frac{2}{3}$ wineglass of whiskey, brandy or Jamaica rum, according to taste; $\frac{1}{3}$ wineglass water; add syrup or other sweetening to suit taste; 1 wineglass of shaved ice. Shake very well, and strain into a fancy cocktail glass.

7

RECIPES

=== FOR MIXING ===

FANCY DRINKS

ANGOSTURA SODA

Large bar glass with two or three lumps of ice; 5 or 6 dashes Angostura Bitters (Dr. Siegert's genuine imported), 1 or 2 slices of orange. Fill up glass with lemon soda and place a teaspoon filled with sugar on top of the glass for customer to put it in himself.

ANGOSTURA GRAPE FRUIT

Cut the fruit in half, extract the core or pithy substance in the center with a sharp knife; insert the knife around the inner edge of the peel and disengage the fruit from the peel without removing the fruit or breaking the peel; sprinkle plentifully with powdered sugar and fill the opening caused by the removal of the core with one-half teaspoon Dr. Siegert's Angostura Bitters (the only genuine). Ice well before serving.

ANGOSTURA LEMON ICE

Four quarts of water, ten lemons, four pounds and a half of sugar and twelve tablespoons (6 oz.) Angostura Bitters (Dr. Siegert's genuine imported). Grate half the lemons, squeeze out, and put rind, juice, half the water and sugar into a pan, set it on the fire and stir until the sugar is dissolved and it becomes quite warm. Then remove and add the remaining two quarts of water and Angostura Bitters and strain into the freezer.

Freeze in the usual manner. Some makers add a few egg whites before freezing or when half frozen; this is not recommended, as it makes the ice too light and the consequence is that the ice will become icy and rough after standing any length of time.

ANGOSTURA JELLY

Allow two heaping teaspoonfuls of gelatine to soak for five minutes in a cup of water; add one quart boiling water, the juice of six lemons, four tablespoons Dr. Siegert's Genuine Imported Angostura Bitters, and sweeten to suit taste. Pour into mould and serve well iced. Use cold boiled custard for sauce. Maraschino cherries make a pleasant addition to this dessert, and may be put in before the jelly is formed.

ANGOSTURA LEMONADE

Add 1 teaspoon Dr. Siegert's Genuine Angostura Bitters to each glass of lemonade.

ANGOSTURA SHERBET

This delightful and popular sherbet is made by adding about a wine glass of Dr. Siegert's Genuine Angostura Bitters to each pint of lemon syrup. To serve use thin glass.

One wine glass of mixture.

Fill up with carbonated water.

ABSINTHE AMERICAN STYLE

A large bar glass.

¾ glass of fine ice.

4 or 5 dashes gum syrup.

1 pony absinthe.

3 wine glasses of water.

Shake the ingredients until the outside of the shaker is covered with ice. Strain into a large bar glass.

Recipes for Mixing Fancy Drinks

ABSINTHE COCKTAIL

Fill mixing glass ⅔ full of fine ice.
1 piece of lemon peel.
3 dashes of syrup.
2 dashes Dr. Siegert's Genuine Angostura Bitters.
¾ wine glass of absinthe.
¼ wine glass of water.
Stir well and strain into a cocktail glass, dash with seltzer, serve.

ABSINTHE DRIPPED

1 pony of absinthe.
Fill the bowl of your absinthe glass (which has a hole in the center) with fine ice and the balance with water. Then elevate the bowl and let contents drip into the glass containing the absinthe until the color shows a sufficiency. Pour into a thin bar glass and serve.

ABSINTHE FRAPPE

Fill mixing glass full of fine ice.
1 teaspoonful of syrup.
1 pony absinthe.
1 wine glass of water.
Shake the ingredients until the outside of glass has frosted appearance, strain into a glass, and fill up with seltzer and serve.

ALE SANGAREE

Fill up ale glass with ale.
1 teaspoonful powdered sugar.
Stir gently, grate a little nutmeg on top and serve.

APOLLINARIS LEMONADE

Fill mixing glass ⅔ full fine ice.
1 tablespoonful of powdered sugar.
The juice of one lemon.

1 split of Apollinaris Water.
Stir the above mixture thoroughly and
strain into a lemonade glass with fruit and
serve.

APPLEJACK COCKTAIL

(Use a large size bar glass.)

¾ glass of fine shaved ice.
2 or 3 dashes of gum syrup.
2 or 3 dashes Dr. Siegert's Genuine Angostura Bitters.
1 or 2 dashes of curaçao.
1 wine glass of applejack.

Stir up well with a spoon and strain it into
a cocktail glass. Put in a cherry or medium-
size olive; squeeze a piece of lemon peel on
top and serve.

APPLE TODDY

(Use hot water glass.)

1 lump of sugar.
1 slice of lemon peel.
Fill the glass ⅔ of boiling water.

Fill up with apple brandy, stir and grate
nutmeg on top. Serve with a spoon.

APPLEJACK SOUR

Fill mixing glass ⅔ full of fine ice.
1 teaspoonful syrup.
1 teaspoonful pineapple syrup.
2 teaspoonfuls lemon juice.
1 wine glass applejack.

Stir well, strain into a sour glass, dash with
seltzer, and serve with fruit.

ASTRINGENT

⅔ wine glass port wine.
⅓ glass French brandy.
3 dashes Dr. Siegert's Genuine Angostura
Bitters.
4 or 5 dashes strong Jamaica ginger.

Stir gently with spoon and serve with a
little nutmeg on top.

11

BARRY COCKTAIL

A very popular drink in 'Frisco.
Place in a small glass a piece of ice.
4 dashes Dr. Siegert's Genuine Angostura
Bitters.
⅓ a jigger of Plymouth gin.
½ a jigger of Italian vermouth.
1 piece of twisted lemon peel.
5 drops of creme de menthe.
Stir it well, strain it into a small bar glass,
and serve with ice water.

BISHOP

Use large bar glass.
1 tablespoon sugar.
2 dashes lemon juice.
½ the juice of an orange.
1 squirt of seltzer water.
Fill up with Burgundy, dash with Jamaica
rum.
2 dashes Dr. Siegert's Genuine Angostura
Bitters.
Stir well, dress with fruit and serve with
straw.

BIJOU COCKTAIL

Use large glass.
¾ glass filled with shaved ice.
⅓ wine glass green chartreuse.
⅓ wine glass Italian vermouth.
⅓ wine glass Plymouth gin.
Stir well with spoon, and after straining in
cocktail glass add cherry or small olive, and
serve after squeezing lemon juice on top.

BLACK STRIPE

Use a whiskey glass, with enough Jamaica
rum to cover bottom of glass.
1 tablespoonful of New Orleans molasses.

Place spoon in glass; hand rum bottle to customer and allow him to stir and help himself.

BLACKTHORNE COCKTAIL

Fill mixing glass ⅔ full fine ice.

1 teaspoonful of syrup.
¼ teaspoonful of lemon juice.
2 dashes orange bitters.
½ wine glass Italian vermouth.
3 dashes Dr. Siegert's Genuine Angostura Bitters.
½ wine glass Sloe gin.

Stir ingredients thoroughly and strain in cocktail glass and serve.

BLUE BLAZER

Use 2 metal mugs or 2 heavy bar glasses.

½ tablespoonful sugar, dissolved in a little water.
1 wine glass of Scotch or Rye whiskey.

Set the liquid on fire, and while blazing pour three or four times from one to the other. This will look like a stream of fire; twist a piece of lemon peel on top, with a little grated nutmeg, and serve. This preparation requires skill; a little practice will be necessary.

BRANDY AND GINGER ALE

Large high glass.
2 or 3 lumps of ice.
1 wine glass of brandy.
1 bottle ginger ale.

Stir with spoon and serve.

BRANDY AND SODA

Large punch glass.
1 or 2 pieces of ice.
1 wine glass of brandy.
1 bottle plain soda.

Stir well and serve. Imported Club Soda is the best to use.

BRANDY BURNED WITH PEACH

Use small bar glass.
1 wine glass of brandy.
½ tablespoon sugar.
Burn brandy and sugar together in a saucer.
Place 2 or 3 slices dried peach in a hot stem glass; pour the burned liquid over it; grate a little nutmeg over it and serve. This is a Southern concoction.

BRANDY CHAMPERELLE

Use a wine glass.
¼ glass curaçao.
¼ glass yellow chartreuse.
¼ glass anisette.
¼ glass brandy.
3 drops Angostura Bitters.
Do not allow colors to mix.

BRANDY COCKTAIL

Mixing glass ⅔ full of fine ice.
3 dashes of plain syrup.
3 dashes Dr. Siegert's Genuine Angostura Bitters.
1 or 2 dashes orange bitters.
1 wine glass brandy.
1 piece of lemon peel.
Stir well and strain into a cocktail glass and serve.

BRANDY CRUSTA

Mixing glass ⅔ full of fine ice.
2 dashes Dr. Siegert's Genuine Angostura Bitters.
3 dashes syrup.
1 dash orange bitters.
1 wine glass brandy.
3 dashes lemon juice.
Stir thoroughly, peel the rind from a lemon all in one piece; fit it into the wine glass, covering the entire inside; rub a slice of lemon

around the top of glass; dip glass into pulverized sugar; strain the mixture into this prepared (tall) glass, and serve.

BRANDY DAISY

A large bar glass half full of ice.
3 or 4 dashes of syrup.
3 dashes curaçao.
3 dashes lemon juice.
1 wine glass brandy.

Shake thoroughly; strain in small thin glass; fill up with seltzer or Apollinaris, and serve.

BRANDY FIX

Use large bar glass, half full of fine ice.
½ teaspoonful sugar.
1 dash of seltzer.
½ pony pineapple syrup.
1 wine glass brandy.
2 dashes Dr. Siegert's Genuine Angostura Bitters.

Stir with spoon; fill up with ice; dress with fruits, and serve with straw.

BRANDY FIZZ

Use large bar glass ⅔ full of ice.
1 teaspoonful of sugar.
3 or 4 dashes of lemon juice.
White of one egg.
1 wine glass of brandy.

Shake well; strain into fizz glass; fill up with seltzer, and drink while effervescing.

BRANDY FLOAT

Use champagne glass.
Fill it ⅔ full of carbonated water.
Use a spoon and float brandy on top.

BRANDY FLIP

Use large bar glass, half full of fine ice.

15

Recipes for Mixing Fancy Drinks

1 whole egg.
½ tablespoon sugar.
1 wine glass brandy.
Shake well and strain into flip glass; grate a little nutmeg on top, and serve.

BRANDY PUNCH

Large bar glass half full of ice.
1 tablespoonful sugar.
1 dash raspberry syrup.
3 dashes lemon juice.
1 dash rum.
1 glass brandy.
2 dashes Dr. Siegert's Genuine Angostura Bitters.
Shake well; fill up with ice; dress with fruit, and serve with straws.

BRANDY SANGAREE

Mixing glass full of ice.
1 teaspoonful of sugar.
½ wine glass mineral water.
1 wine glass brandy.
1 dash Dr. Siegert's Genuine Angostura Bitters.
Stir well; dash port wine on top; grate nutmeg, and serve.

BRANDY SCAFFA

Use sherry glass.
¼ glass raspberry syrup.
¼ glass maraschino.
¼ glass green chartreuse.
Top off with brandy and serve like Pousse Cafe.

BRANDY SMASH

Use old-fashioned cocktail glass.
1 teaspoonful sugar dissolved with seltzer.
3 or 4 sprigs of mint pressed slightly with muddler.

1 good sized piece of ice.
1 wine glass brandy.
1 dash Dr. Siegert's Genuine Angostura
Bitters.

Stir well; dash with seltzer, and serve with spoon in the glass.

BRANDY SOUR

Use mixing glass ⅔ full of ice.
3 dashes syrup
3 dashes lemon juice.
1 wine glass brandy.

Stir well; strain into small thin glass with pineapple and dash with seltzer, and serve.

BRANDY TODDY

Put in a whiskey glass:
1 teaspoonful of sugar dissolved in a little water.
1 small piece of ice.

Hand the bottle of brandy to the customer and let him help himself.

BRUT COCKTAIL

Use mixing glass full of shaved ice.
6 dashes Dr. Siegert's Genuine Angostura
Bitters.
⅓ glass Amer Picon.
⅔ glass of French Vermouth.

Stir well; strain into a cocktail glass, and serve.

CALIFORNIA SHERRY COBBLER

Large bar glass half full of ice.
½ tablespoonful of sugar.
1 pony pineapple syrup.
1 wine glass California sherry.
1 dash Dr. Siegert's Genuine Angostura
Bitters.

Stir well; fill up with ice; dress with fruit; dash port wine on top; serve with a straw.

Recipes for Mixing Fancy Drinks

CHAMPAGNE AND CLARET CUP

Use large punch bowl.
4 bottles of claret wine.
1 pint of curaçao.
1 pint of sherry.
1 quart of French brandy.
½ pint raspberry syrup.
3 jiggers Dr. Siegert's Genuine Angostura Bitters.
4 oranges, sliced.
3 lemons, sliced.
3 bottles carbonated water.
2 bottles sweet soda.

Sweeten with granulated sugar; then let it stand two hours; place large square of ice in bowl; it is then fit for use. This will serve thirty-five persons, using glass cups.

CHAMPAGNE COBBLER

Use medium sized thin glass.
⅓ full of shaved ice.
1 teaspoon powdered sugar.
1 piece each of orange and lemon peel.

Fill with wine; decorate with berries, and serve with straw. One quart of wine will serve four or five persons.

CHAMPAGNE COCKTAIL

Use tall thin glass.
1 lump of sugar.
2 dashes Dr. Siegert's Genuine Angostura Bitters.
1 small lump of ice.
1 piece of twisted lemon peel.

Fill up glass with wine; stir up with a spoon, and serve. One pint of wine will make three drinks; one quart will make six cocktails.

CHAMPAGNE CUP

For a four-gallon mixture put in a large punch bowl:
2 cans pineapple, quartered.
8 oranges, sliced.
4 lemons, sliced.
1 quart curaçao.
1 pint chartreuse.
1 pint abricotine.
1 quart Cognac brandy.
1 quart of Tokay or Catawba wine.
½ small bottle Dr. Siegert's Genuine Angostura Bitters.

Stir up well and let it stand over night, and add, when ready to use, 3 quarts Apollinaris, 6 quarts champagne; put a large piece of ice in the punch bowl; decorate with fruits, and serve in champagne cups.

CHAMPAGNE JULEP

Use mixing glass half full of ice.
1 lump of white sugar.
3 sprigs of mint.

Pour wine into glass slowly; stir gently; fill up with ice; dress with fruits; dash brandy on top and serve with straw.

CHAMPAGNE PUNCH

Put in a large punch bowl.
4 quarts champagne.
2 quarts mineral water.
2 jiggers Dr. Siegert's Genuine Angostura Bitters.
8 pieces cut loaf sugar.
3 oranges, sliced.
3 lemons, sliced.
1 can pineapple, sliced and quartered.
1 pint abricotine.

Stir gently and place large square of ice in bowl; serve in glass cups.

CHAMPAGNE SOUR

Use fancy sour glass.
1 lump sugar.

3 dashes of lemon juice.
Fill the glass slowly with champagne.
Stir gently; dress with fruit and serve.

CHAMPAGNE VELVET

For this drink a bottle of champagne and a bottle of porter (both cold) must be used. Fill the goblet half full of porter and balance with champagne; stir with a spoon slowly and carefully, and serve.

CHOCOLATE PUNCH

Use large bar glass ⅔ full of fine ice.
½ tablespoon sugar.
1 wine glass port wine.
1 pony curaçao.
1 egg, and fill glass with milk.
Shake thoroughly; strain into a punch glass and grate a little nutmeg on top and serve.

CINCINNATI COCKTAIL

½ glass of beer; fill up with soda or ginger ale. This is a palatable drink for warm weather.

CLARET COBBLER

Use mixing glass half full of fine ice.
1 teaspoon sugar.
3 pieces lemon peel.
2 wine glasses claret.
2 dashes Dr. Siegert's Genuine Angostura Bitters.
Stir gently; fill up with ice; dress with fruits, and serve with straws.

CLARET CUP

Put in punch bowl for two-gallon mixture:

1 can pineapple.
4 oranges, sliced.
3 lemons, sliced.
3 wine glasses abricotine.
2 wine glasses curaçao.
3 jiggers Dr. Siegert's Genuine Angostura Bitters.
2 quart bottles mineral water.
4 quart bottles of claret.

Let this mixture stand about four hours; then put a large piece of ice in bowl; add 2 quarts champagne, or other sparkling wine; decorate the ice with fruits, and serve in champagne glasses.

CLARET LEMONADE

(Use a large bar glass.)

¾ tablespoonful of sugar.
6 to 8 dashes of lemon juice.

Fill tumbler nearly full with fine-shaved ice, and the balance with water; shake up well with a shaker, ornament with fruits in season and top it off with
1 dash Dr. Siegert's Genuine Angostura Bitters.

½ glass of claret wine; be careful to have the claret flowing on top of lemonade, and serve with a straw.

CLARET PUNCH

Use large bar glass. ⅔ full fine ice.
1 tablespoon sugar.
3 or 4 dashes lemon juice.
2 wine glasses claret.

Shake well; strain in thin glass; dash with seltzer; dress with fruits, and serve with straws.

COFFEE COCKTAIL

Use large bar glass ⅔ full of ice.
1 teaspoon sugar.
1 fresh egg.
1 wine glass port wine.
1 pony brandy.

21

Recipes for Mixing Fancy Drinks

Shake thoroughly; strain into medium-sized thin glass; grate a little nutmeg on top, and serve.

CURAÇAO PUNCH

Use large bar glass half full of ice.
1 tablespoon powdered sugar.
3 or 4 dashes lemon juice.
½ wine glass brandy.
1 pony curaçao.
½ pony Jamaica rum.
3 dashes Dr. Siegert's Genuine Angostura Bitters.
½ glass carbonated water.

Stir well with spoon; fill up with ice; dress with fruits; serve with straws.

EGG LEMONADE

Use large bar glass ⅔ full of fine ice.
1 tablespoon powdered sugar.
Juice of one lemon.
1 fresh egg.

Fill up glass with water; shake thoroughly; strain into a thin lemonade glass, and serve.

EGGNOG

Use large bar glass half full of ice.
1 fresh egg.
½ tablespoon sugar.
½ pony Jamaica rum.
1 pony brandy.

Fill up the glass with rich milk and shake up well until thoroughly mixed; strain into a tall, thin glass and grate nutmeg on top, and serve.

FANCY WHISKEY SMASH

Use large bar glass half full of ice.
2 teaspoons sugar.
1 wine glass carbonated water

3 sprigs of mint, pressed.
1 wine glass whiskey.
Stir well; fill up with ice; trim with fruit, and serve.

FISH HOUSE PUNCH

⅓ pint lemon juice.
¾ pound white sugar, dissolved in sufficient water.
½ pint Cognac brandy.
¼ pint peach brandy
¼ pint Jamaica rum.
4 tablespoons Dr. Siegert's Genuine Angostura Bitters.
2½ pints cold water.

Ice and serve.

GIN AND BITTERS

OR

GIN AND ANGOSTURA

Serve the same as Sherry and Angostura, substituting gin for sherry.

GIN AND CALAMUS

Use whiskey glass.

2 or 3 small pieces of Calamus root should be placed in a bottle of gin until the essence has been extracted. To serve, hand out glass with the bottle; allow customer to help himself.

GIN AND MILK

Use whiskey glass.
Hand out glass with spoon in and the bottle of gin; allow customer to help himself, then fill up glass with cold milk.

GIN AND MOLASSES

Use whiskey glass.
Put enough gin in glass to cover the bottom; drop in one tablespoon of New Orleans

molasses; place spoon in glass, and allow customer to help himself from gin bottle. Use hot water to cleanse glass.

GIN AND TANSY

Use whiskey glass.
This is an old-fashioned and excellent tonic. It is prepared by steeping a bunch of tansy in a bottle of Holland gin, which will extract the essence; when serving, set the glass, with the lump of ice, before the customer, allowing him to help himself.

GIN COCKTAIL

Fill mixing glass ⅔ full of ice.
1 piece of lemon peel.
1 teaspoon of syrup.
2 dashes of orange bitters.
2 dashes Dr. Siegert's Genuine Angostura Bitters.
1 wine glass of gin.

Stir and strain in cocktail glass, with fruit, if desired.

GIN CRUSTA

Prepare this drink like a Brandy Crusta, using gin in place of brandy.

GIN DAISY

Prepare this drink in the same manner as Brandy Daisy, substituting gin for brandy.

GIN FIX

Use large bar glass, half full of ice.
½ tablespoon of sugar.
½ pony pineapple syrup.
1 wine glass Holland gin.

Dash with seltzer.
Fill glass with ice; dress with fruit, and
serve with straw.

GIN FIZZ

(Plain)

Use large bar glass ⅔ full of ice.
½ tablespoon of sugar.
3 or 4 dashes lemon juice.
1 jigger Old Tom gin.
Shake well; strain into fizz glass; fill up
with seltzer.

GIN FIZZ

(Golden)

Use large bar glass ⅔ full of ice.
½ tablespoon of sugar.
3 or 4 dashes of lemon juice.
3 dashes Angostura Bitters.
1 jigger Old Tom Gin.
1 fresh egg.
Shake well; strain into fizz glass; fill up
with seltzer.

GIN FIZZ

(Silver)

Use large bar glass ⅔ full of ice.
½ tablespoon of sugar.
3 or 4 dashes of lemon juice
1 jigger Old Tom Gin.
White of one egg.
Shake well; strain into fizz glass; fill up
with seltzer.

GIN FLIP

Use large bar glass ½ full of ice.
1 teaspoon sugar, with dash of seltzer.
1 wine glass Holland gin.
1 fresh egg.
Shake well; strain in fancy glass; grate
nutmeg on top, and serve.

GIN JULEP

Use a large bar glass.
¾ tablespoonful of sugar.

Recipes for Mixing Fancy Drinks

3 or 4 sprigs of mint.

½ wine glass of water, dissolve well, until the essence of the mint is extracted, then remove the mint.

Fill up with fine ice.

1 ¼ wine glass of Holland gin.

1 dash Dr. Siegert's Genuine Angostura Bitters.

Stir up well with a spoon, ornament it the same as mint julep and serve.

GIN PUNCH

Use large bar glass ½ full of ice.

1 tablespoon raspberry syrup.

1 tablespoon powdered sugar, dissolved in seltzer.

1 ½ wine glass of Holland gin.

3 or 4 dashes lemon juice.

1 slice of orange, cut up.

2 dashes maraschino.

Fill up with ice; shake well, and dress with pineapple and berries.

GIN RICKEY

Take a rickey glass.

Juice of one lemon or lime.

1 nicely cut piece of ice.

Place whiskey glass on bar beside bottle; allow customer to help himself; put drink into the rickey glass; fill up with seltzer or other mineral water; place spoon in glass; serve.

GIN SANGAREE

Prepare this drink same as Brandy Sangaree, substituting gin instead of brandy.

GIN SMASH

Use old-fashioned cocktail glass.

1 teaspoon powdered sugar.

1 dash of seltzer.

4 or 5 sprigs of mint.

Crush the mint slightly with muddler and fill up glass with cracked ice; add one jigger of gin; stir gently; and serve with a spoon.

GIN SOUR

Use a large bar glass.

½ tablespoon of sugar.

2 or 3 dashes of lemon juice.

1 dash of lime juice.

1 squirt of seltzer.

Dissolve the sugar and lemon well with a spoon.

¾ of a wine glass filled with finely shaved ice.

1 wine glass of Holland gin.

Mix well, strain it into a sour glass, dress with a little fruit in season, and serve.

GIN TODDY

Use a whiskey glass.

½ teaspoon of sugar, dissolve well in a little water.

1 or 2 lumps of broken ice.

1 wine glass Holland gin.

Stir up well, and serve.

The proper way to serve this drink is to dissolve the sugar with a little water, put the spoon and ice into the glass, and hand out the bottle of liquor to the customer to help himself.

GUM SYRUP

Take 15 pounds loaf or granulated sugar.

1 gallon of water.

Boil for 8 or 10 minutes; then add enough water to make 2 gallons.

27

Recipes for Mixing Fancy Drinks

HALF AND HALF

Mix half ale or beer and porter together.
This is the American style.

HIGH BALL

Place in a high ball glass:
1 piece of nicely cut ice.
1 fresh piece of lemon peel.
Place a glass and bottle on bar for customer to help himself; then pour the liquor in high ball glass and fill up with seltzer, or any water the customer may desire; place spoon in glass, and serve.

HOCK COBBLER

Prepared same as Claret Cobbler; substitute Hock wine instead.

HONOLULU COCKTAIL

Use star champagne glass.
1 small piece of ice.
3 dashes Dr. Siegert's Genuine Angostura Bitters.
1 jigger whiskey.
Fill almost to top of glass with seltzer; then drop in small spoon of sugar and stir; drink while effervescing.

HORSE'S NECK

Use large size fizz glass.
Peel a whole lemon in one long string and place in glass so one end hangs over edge.
2 or 3 lumps of ice.
Fill up glass with imported ginger ale and serve.

HOT LEMONADE

Use a large bar glass.

1 tablespoonful of sugar.
7 or 8 dashes of lemon juice.

Fill up the glass with hot water; stir up with a spoon and serve.

It is always necessary to pour a little hot water into the glass at first and stir a little, to prevent the glass from cracking, and also place a little fine ice in a separate glass in case the drink should be too hot; in order to make this drink palatable, sugar and lemon should not be spared.

HOT RUM

Use hot water glass.

1 lump of sugar.
Hot water enough to dissolve sugar.
1 wine glass Jamaica rum.

Fill with hot water; put in fresh lemon peel; stir, and grate nutmeg on top.

HOT SPICED RUM

Prepare same as hot rum; add cloves and allspice, and dash with Dr. Siegert's Genuine Angostura Bitters.

HOT WHISKEY SLING

Use hot water glass.

1 lump of sugar and enough hot water to dissolve it.
1 wine glass whiskey.
1 piece lemon peel.

Fill up glass with hot water; stir with spoon; grate nutmeg on top.

HOT SCOTCH WHISKEY

Prepare the same as above, substituting Scotch whiskey.

Recipes for Mixing Fancy Drinks

HOT IRISH WHISKEY

Prepare the same as above, substituting Irish whiskey.

HOT WHISKEY PUNCH

Use hot water punch glass.
Rinse glass in hot water and then put in 2 lumps of sugar and enough hot water to dissolve them.
1 piece lemon peel.
3 or 4 dashes of lemon juice.
1 jigger of whiskey.
Fill up with hot water, stir with spoon, grate nutmeg on top, and serve.

HOT SCOTCH WHISKEY PUNCH

Prepare the same as hot whiskey punch, using Scotch whiskey instead.

HOT IRISH PUNCH

Prepare the same as above, using Irish whiskey instead.

HOT RUM PUNCH

Prepare the same as whiskey punch, substituting rum for whiskey.

JAPANESE COCKTAIL

Use large bar glass half full of ice.
3 or 4 dashes Orgeat syrup.
2 dashes Dr. Siegert's Genuine Angostura Bitters.
1 jigger of brandy.
Stir well; strain into cocktail glass and serve.

JERSEY COCKTAIL

Use mixing glass half full of ice.

1 teaspoon sugar.
2 or 3 dashes of Dr. Siegert's Genuine Angostura Bitters.
1 jigger of cider.

Stir well; strain into a cocktail glass and twist lemon peel on top.

JERSEY LILY POUSSE CAFE

Use pony glass.

½ green Chartreuse.
½ Cognac Brandy.
10 drops Dr. Siegert's Genuine Angostura Bitters.

Pour brandy in carefully so it will not mix, and serve.

JERSEY SUNSET

Into a straight champagne glass put a scant teaspoonful of sugar with enough water to dissolve. Add a twist of lemon or lime peel and half a whiskey glass of fine Old Monmouth Applejack. Now put in enough broken ice to cool, fill with water and finish with a dash or two of Dr. Siegert's Genuine Angostura Bitters, which should not be stirred in, but be allowed to drop slowly through the amber mixture, imparting to it the sunset hues that probably suggested its name.

In winter, instead of ice, hot water is used, making a most genial drink—A Hot Sunset.

JOHN COLLINS

Use large bar glass.

½ dozen lumps of ice.
1 teaspoon fine sugar.
2 or 3 dashes of lemon juice.
1 jigger of Tom gin.
1 bottle plain soda.

31

Recipes for Mixing Fancy Drinks

Mix well with spoon; take out spoon and serve.

KIRSCHWASSER PUNCH

Use large bar glass half full of ice.
1 or 2 dashes lime or lemon juice.
½ tablespoon powdered sugar.
3 dashes yellow Chartreuse.
1 dash seltzer.
1 glass Kirschwasser.
Stir well; fill up with ice; trim with fruit; serve with straws.

KNICKERBEIN

Use sherry wine glass.
⅓ raspberry cordial.
1 yolk of an egg.
Cover egg with Benedictine.
⅓ glass Kummel.
6 drops of Dr. Siegert's Genuine Angostura Bitters.
Prepare this drink as you would when making a Pousse Cafe so that the colors will keep separate.

KNICKERBOCKER

Use large bar glass.
4 or 5 dashes of raspberry syrup.
4 or 5 dashes lemon juice.
1 slice pineapple.
1 slice of orange.
1 slice of lemon.
1 jigger of Santa Cruz Rum.
1 dash Dr. Siegert's Genuine Angostura Bitters.
3 dashes of Curaçao.
Fill up glass with ice; stir well; trim with fruit, and serve.

LEMONADE

Use large bar glass, half full of-ice.
1 heaping tablespoon of sugar.

6 or 8 dashes of lemon juice.

Fill up with water; shake well; dress with fruit; serve with straw. When customer wishes lemonade strained, put into smaller glass and place slice of orange in glass.

An Angostura Lemonade is made like the foregoing with the addition of 1 teaspoon Dr. Siegert's Genuine Angostura Bitters.

MAMIE TAYLOR

A half whiskey glass of Old Monmouth Applejack in a straight champagne glass; fill with cold ginger ale. It is very good and refreshing, and so simple that one feels that he thought of it himself. By W. A. French.

MANHATTAN COCKTAIL

Use mixing glass half full of ice.

1 piece of lemon peel.

1 dash syrup.

2 dashes Dr. Siegert's Genuine Angostura Bitters.

1 dash of orange bitters.

½ jigger of Vermouth.

½ jigger of whiskey.

Stir well; strain into cocktail glass and serve.

MARTINEZ COCKTAIL

Prepare same as Manhattan Cocktail, substituting gin for whiskey.

MAY WINE PUNCH

Use a large punch bowl.

Take one or two bunches of (Waldmeister) Woodruff, and cut it up in two or three lengths, place it into a large bar glass, and fill up the balance with French brandy, cover it up and let it stand for two or three hours, until the essence of the Woodruff is thoroughly extracted; cover the bottom of the bowl with loaf sugar, and pour from

4 to 6 bottles of plain soda water over the sugar.

Cut up 6 oranges in slices.

½ pineapple, and sufficient berries and grapes.

8 bottles of Rhine or Moselle wine.

1 bottle of champagne.

3 jiggers Dr. Siegert's Genuine Angostura Bitters.

Then put your Woodruff and brandy, etc., into the bowl, and stir up with the ladle.

Surround the bowl with ice, serve in a wine glass in such a manner that each customer will get a piece of all the fruits contained in the punch.

MILK PUNCH

Use large bar glass half full of ice.

1 tablespoon fine sugar.

½ jigger Cognac Brandy.

½ jigger rum.

Fill up with milk; shake well; strain into tall thin glass; grate nutmeg on top, and serve.

Angostura Milk Punch is made as the foregoing with 2 dashes Dr. Siegert's Genuine Angostura Bitters on top.

MILK PUNCH (HOT)

Prepare this punch same as milk punch, using hot milk and omit ice.

MILK SHAKE

Use large bar glass half full of ice.

1 tablespoon sugar.

1 fresh egg.

Fill up with milk; shake well, and strain

into tall thin glass; grate nutmeg on top, and serve.

MINT JULEP

Use large bar glass.

Take 3 or 4 sprigs of fresh mint.
1 tablespoon sugar.
1 dash mineral water.

Press mint well in the sugar and water, until the flavor is extracted; add 1 ½ jiggers of brandy; fill up glass with fine shaved ice, then draw out the sprigs of mint, and place them with stems downward in ice; dress with berries and sliced fruit; dash with Jamaica rum, and serve with straws.

MINT JULEP

(Southern Style.)

Use large bar glass.

6 or 8 sprigs of fresh mint.
1 teaspoon fine sugar.
2 dashes Dr. Siegert's Genuine Angostura Bitters.
½ wine glass carbonated water.
½ wine glass peach brandy.
½ wine glass Cognac brandy.

Fill up glass with shaved ice; stir with spoon; dress with sprigs of mint, and serve with straws.

MISSISSIPPI PUNCH

Use large bar glass.

1 tablespoon sugar.
Enough water to dissolve the sugar.
3 or 4 dashes lemon juice.
2 dashes Dr. Siegert's Genuine Angostura Bitters.
½ wine glass Jamaica rum.
½ wine glass Bourbon whiskey.
½ wine glass brandy.

Mix well; fill up with ice; trim with fruit; serve with straws.

Recipes for Mixing Fancy Drinks

MONTANA CLUB COCKTAIL

Use large bar glass, half full of ice.
2 dashes Dr. Siegert's Genuine Angostura Bitters.
2 dashes Anisette.
½ jigger French vermouth.
½ jigger California brandy.
Stir with spoon; strain in cocktail glass; put in olive, and serve.

MORNING GLORY FIZZ

Use large bar glass full of ice.
2 or 3 dashes of gum syrup.
2 dashes of lime or lemon juice.
2 dashes curaçao.
2 dashes Dr. Siegert's Genuine Angostura Bitters.
2 dashes of Absinthe.
½ jigger of brandy.
½ jigger of whiskey.
Shake well; strain in tall thin glass; fill up with seltzer or any other water desired; this is a good bracer in the morning.

MULLED CLARET

1 lump of sugar.
¼ teaspoon cinnamon.
¼ teaspoon fine cloves.
½ teaspoon fine allspice.
3 or 4 dashes of lemon juice.
2 dashes Dr. Siegert's Genuine Angostura Bitters.
2 jiggers of claret.
Use a large bar glass; heat a poker red hot and stick into liquid until it boils; strain, and serve in hot claret.

OLD FASHIONED COCKTAIL

Use old fashioned cocktail glass.
1 piece cut of loaf sugar.
Dash with seltzer and crush sugar with muddler.
1 dash of orange bitters.
1 square piece of ice.
3 dashes Dr. Siegert's Genuine Angostura Bitters.
1 piece of lemon peel.
1 jigger whiskey.
Stir gently, and serve with spoon in glass.

OLD FASHIONED TODDY

Use old fashioned cocktail glass.
1 teaspoon sugar with dash of seltzer.
2 or 3 small pieces of ice.
1 jigger of Old Bourbon Whiskey.
Stir gently, and serve with spoon in glass.

OLD TOM GIN COCKTAIL

Use mixing glass half full of ice.
3 dashes Dr. Siegert's Genuine Angostura Bitters.
2 dashes curaçao.
2 dashes gum syrup.
1 jigger Old Tom Gin.
Stir well; strain into a cocktail glass; twist lemon peel on top.

OLIVETTE COCKTAIL

Use large bar glass half full of ice.
2 dashes syrup.
3 dashes orange bitters.
3 dashes Absinthe.
1 dash Dr. Siegert's Genuine Angostura Bitters.
1 jigger Plymouth Gin.
Stir with spoon; strain in cocktail glass; put in olive; twist lemon peel on top, and serve.

27

Recipes for Mixing Fancy Drinks

ORGEAT PUNCH

Use large bar glass half full of ice.
½ jigger Orgeat syrup.
1 jigger French Brandy.
4 or 5 dashes lemon juice.
Stir well; fill up with ice; dash with port wine; trim with fruit; and serve.

OYSTER COCKTAIL

Use star champagne glass.
½ dozen small oysters.
1 dash lemon juice.
3 dashes Paprika Sauce.
2 dashes vinegar.
1 dash Tabasco Sauce.
Shake on top a little salt and pepper.
Stir gently with spoon, and serve.

PALMETTO COCKTAIL

Mixing glass half full of ice.
3 dashes Dr. Siegert's Genuine Angostura Bitters.
½ jigger Santa Cruz rum.
½ jigger Vermouth.
Stir well; strain into cocktail glass, and serve.

PARISIAN POUSSE CAFE

Use Pousse Cafe glass.
2-5 Curaçao.
2-5 Kirschwasser.
1-5 Chartreuse.
A celebrated drink in Paris.

PEACH AND HONEY

Use whiskey glass.
1 tablespoon pure honey.
1 jigger peach brandy.
Stir with spoon, and serve.

Continued on Page 39

Recipes for Mixing Fancy Drinks

PINEAPPLE JULEP

For a party of 6 use a small punch bowl.
1 quart of sparkling Moselle.
1 jigger raspberry syrup.
1 jigger Maraschino.
1 jigger DeKuyper gin.
1 jigger of lemon juice.
1 jigger orange bitters.
1 jigger Dr. Siegert's Genuine Angostura Bitters.
4 oranges, sliced.
2 lemons, sliced.
1 ripe pineapple, sliced and quartered.
4 tablespoons sugar.
1 bottle Apollinaris water.
Place large square of ice in bowl; dress with the fruits, and serve julep in fancy stem glass.

PORT WINE COBBLER

Use large bar glass half full of ice.
½ jigger Orchard syrup.
½ tablespoonful sugar.
1 jigger port wine.
1 dash Dr. Siegert's Genuine Angostura Bitters.
Stir well; fill up with ice; dress with fruit; serve with straw.

PORT WINE FLIP

Use large bar glass, half full of ice.
½ tablespoon sugar.
1 jigger of port wine.
1 fresh egg.
Shake well, strain in flip glass, grate nutmeg on top, and serve.

PORT WINE PUNCH

Use large bar glass, half full ice.
4 dashes lemon juice.
4 dashes Orchard syrup.
1 tablespoon sugar.

Recipes for Mixing Fancy Drinks

2 jiggers port wine.

2 dashes Dr. Siegert's Genuine Angostura Bitters.

Stir well; fill up with ice; dress with fruit, and serve with straws.

PORT WINE SANGAREE

Use large bar glass, half full of ice.

1 teaspoon sugar.

1 large glass of port wine.

Shake well; strain in fancy stem glass; grate nutmeg on top, and serve.

POUSSE CAFE

Pour in pousse cafe glass as follows:

$\frac{1}{6}$ glass raspberry syrup.

$\frac{1}{6}$ glass Maraschino.

$\frac{1}{6}$ glass green vanilla.

$\frac{1}{6}$ glass curaçao.

$\frac{1}{6}$ glass yellow chartreuse.

$\frac{1}{6}$ glass brandy.

In preparing the above use a small wine glass with spoon, for pouring in each cordial separately. Be careful they do not mix together.

POUSSE CAFE

$\frac{1}{2}$ glass Maraschino.

$\frac{1}{8}$ glass vanilla.

$\frac{1}{8}$ glass curaçao.

$\frac{1}{8}$ glass chartreuse.

$\frac{1}{8}$ glass brandy.

This is the Parisian Cafe recipe. Serve without letting colors mix.

POUSSE CAFE

(Manhattan).

$\frac{1}{4}$ Maraschino.

$\frac{1}{4}$ curaçao.

¼ green chartreuse.
¼ brandy.

This is the New York Cafe style of serving.
Don't allow colors to mix.

POUSSE L'AMOUR

Use sherry glass.
¼ glass Maraschino.
Yolk of 1 egg.
¼ glass vanilla cordial.
¼ glass brandy.
Keep this drink in separate layers and
serve.

PUNCH A LA ROMAINE

1 bottle champagne.
1 bottle rum.
2 tablespoons Dr. Siegert's Genuine Angostura Bitters.
10 lemons.
3 sweet oranges.
2 pounds powdered sugar.
10 fresh eggs.
For a party of 15.
Dissolve the sugar in the juice of the lemons
and oranges, adding the rind of one orange;
strain through a sieve into a bowl, and add
by degrees the whites of the eggs, beaten to
a froth. Place the bowl on ice till cold, then
stir in the rum and wine until thoroughly
mixed. Serve in fancy stem glasses.

REGENT PUNCH

To one and one-half pints of strong, hot
green tea add one and one-half pints of lemon
juice, one and one-half pints of Capillaire,
one pint Jamaica rum, one pint brandy, one
pint Batavia arrack, one pint curaçao, one
bottle champagne, 2 tablespoons Dr. Siegert's
Genuine Angostura Bitters, one sliced pine-

apple, and two sliced oranges. Mix thoroughly in a punch bowl. Add the wine and ice just before serving.

REMSEN COOLER

Use a medium size fizz glass.
Peel a lemon as you would an apple.
Place the rind or peeling into the fizz glass.
2 or 3 lumps of crystal ice.
1 wine glass of Remsen Scotch whiskey.
Fill up the balance with club soda.
Stir up slowly with a spoon and serve.

In this country it is often the case that people call a Remsen cooler where they want Old Tom gin or Sloe gin, instead of Scotch whiskey; it is therefore the bartender's duty to mix as desired.

RENAUD'S POUSSE CAFE

$\frac{1}{3}$ Cognac brandy.
$\frac{1}{3}$ Maraschino.
$\frac{1}{3}$ Curaçao.

Put in whiskey glass; mix well with spoon; withdraw spoon, and serve. This delightful drink is from a recipe by Renaud of New Orleans.

RHINE WINE COBBLER

Use large bar glass, half full of ice.
1 tablespoon of sugar.
1 jigger mineral water.
2 jiggers Rhine wine.

Fill up with ice; stir well; ornament with fruit, and serve with straws.

RHINE WINE CUP

is made the same as Claret Cup, except that
Rhine wine is used instead of claret.

RHINE WINE LEMONADE

Use large bar glass.
1 tablespoon sugar.
Juice of one orange.
½ glass of ice.
Fill up with Rhine wine.
Stir well; add slice of orange with straws,
and serve.

ROB ROY COCKTAIL

Use mixing glass half full of ice.
3 dashes of lemon juice.
2 dashes syrup.
2 dashes orange bitters.
2 dashes Dr. Siegert's Genuine Angostura
Bitters.
    ½ jigger Scotch whiskey.
    ½ jigger French Vermouth.
Stir well; strain into a cocktail glass with
olive or cherry, and serve.

ROCK AND RYE

Put in half tablespoon of rock candy syrup,
and allow customer to serve himself from rye
whiskey bottle.   Put spoon in glass.

ROMAN PUNCH

Use large bar glass.
1 tablespoon sugar.
1 tablespoon raspberry syrup.
1 tablespoon lemon juice.
1 jigger carbonated water.
Juice of half an orange.
1 teaspoon curaçao.
½ teaspoon Dr. Siegert's Genuine Angostura Bitters.
    ½ jigger brandy.

Recipes for Mixing Fancy Drinks

½ jigger Jamaica rum.
Fill up glass with ice; stir well; dash with port wine; trim with fruit, and serve with straws.

ROYAL PUNCH

1 pint hot green tea.
½ pint brandy.
½ pint Jamaica rum.
1 jigger arrack.
1 jigger curaçao.
1 jigger Dr. Siegert's Genuine Angostura Bitters.
Juice of 3 limes.
1 lemon, sliced.
1 cup warm calf's-foot jelly.
1 cup sugar.
Mix well, while heating, and drink as hot as possible.   For party of six.

RUM FLIP

Prepare this drink same as gin flip, using Jamaica rum instead of gin.

RUM FLIP

(Western Style.)

½ pint of ale, heated on fire.
1 egg beaten up with powdered sugar.
Put the ale in one cup, the egg in another with a small jigger of rum or brandy; pour from one cup into another several times until thoroughly mixed, dash nutmeg on top and serve.

RUM DAISY

Mixing glass ½ full of ice.
3 dashes of syrup.
3 dashes of lemon.
3 dashes orange bitters.

½ jigger rum.
1 jigger mineral water.
Stir well, strain into thin glass, fill up with carbonated water.

SARATOGA COCKTAIL

Use mixing glass half full of ice.
3 dashes Dr. Siegert's Genuine Angostura Bitters.
⅓ jigger brandy.
⅓ jigger whiskey.
⅓ jigger Vermouth.
Stir well, strain into a claret glass and serve, with slice of lemon.

SAUTERNE COBBLER

Use large bar glass half full of ice.
½ jigger Orchard syrup.
2 jiggers Sauterne.
Stir well, fill up with ice, dress with fruit, serve with a straw.

SELTZER LEMONADE

Use large bar glass.
5 or 6 dashes lemon juice.
1 tablespoon sugar.
2 or 3 lumps of ice.
Fill up with seltzer, stir with spoon and serve.

SHANDY GAFF

Use a large bar glass.
Fill half the glass with porter and half the glass with ginger ale.
It is also made with half ale and half ginger ale.

SHERRY AND ANGOSTURA

Put 2 dashes Dr. Siegert's Genuine Angostura Bitters in a sherry glass and roll the glass till the bitters entirely covers the inside surface.
Fill the glass with sherry and serve.

Recipes for Mixing Fancy Drinks

SHERRY AND EGG

Use a whiskey glass.

In preparing the above drink, place a small portion of sherry wine into the glass, barely enough to cover the bottom, to prevent the egg from sticking to the glass, then break a fresh ice-cold egg into it, hand this out to the customer and also the bottle of sherry wine to help himself.

SHERRY COBBLER

Large bar glass half full of ice.

1 tablespoon sugar.
2 or 3 slices of orange.
2 jiggers of sherry.
2 dashes Dr. Siegert's Genuine Angostura Bitters.

Shake well, fill up with ice, dress top with fruit and serve with straw.

SHERRY COCKTAIL

Use a large bar glass.

¾ glassful of shaved ice.
2 or 3 dashes Dr. Siegert's Genuine Angostura Bitters.
1 dash of Maraschino.
1 wine glass of sherry wine.

Stir up well with spoon; strain into a cocktail glass, put a cherry into it, squeeze a piece of lemon peel on top, and serve.

SHERRY WINE FLIP

Large bar glass half full of ice.

1 fresh egg.
½ tablespoon sugar.
1½ jiggers sherry.

Shake well, strain into fancy glass, grate nutmeg on top and serve.

SHERRY WINE PUNCH

Use a large bar glass.
½ wine glass of orchard syrup.
1 dash of lemon juice.
2 dashes Dr. Siegert's Genuine Angostura Bitters.
Fill the glass with fine shaved ice.
1 ½ wine glasses sherry.

Stir up well with a spoon; ornament with grapes, oranges, pineapples and berries; top it off with a little claret wine, and serve with a straw.

SHERRY WINE SANGAREE

Prepare this drink same as Port Wine Sangaree, substituting sherry for port.

SILVER COCKTAIL

Use mixing glass half full of ice.

1 dash gum syrup.
2 dashes orange bitters.
1 dash Dr. Siegert's Genuine Angostura Bitters.
2 dashes Maraschino.
½ jigger French Vermouth.
½ jigger Gordon Gin.

Stir well, strain in cocktail glass, twist lemon peel on top and serve.

SLOE GIN FIZZ

Use large bar glass half full of ice.

3 dashes lemon juice.
½ tablespoon sugar.
1 jigger Sloe Gin.
3 dashes Angostura Bitters.

Shake well, strain into fizz glass, fill up with seltzer and serve.

SODA COCKTAIL

Large bar glass with 2 or 3 lumps of ice.

1 teaspoon sugar.
2 or 3 dashes Dr. Siegert's Genuine Angostura Bitters.

47

Recipes for Mixing Fancy Drinks

Fill up glass with lemon soda, stir well, and serve.

SODA LEMONADE

Prepare this drink same as Seltzer Lemonade, substituting soda for seltzer.

SODA NEGUS

Use small punch bowl.

1 pint of port wine.
½ tablespoon of Dr. Siegert's Genuine Angostura Bitters.
12 lumps loaf sugar.
12 cloves.
1 teaspoon nutmeg.

Put above ingredients into a clean saucepan, warm and stir well, do not let it boil, pour in on this mixture 1 bottle plain soda. Put in punch bowl, and serve in cups.

STAR COCKTAIL

Use large bar glass half full of ice.

2 dashes gum syrup.
1 dash Curaçao.
2 dashes Dr. Siegert's Genuine Angostura Bitters.
½ jigger French Vermouth.
½ jigger of Applejack.

Stir with spoon, strain in cocktail glass, add cherry and serve.

STONE FENCE

Use whiskey glass and 2 small pieces of ice.

Place spoon in glass and allow customer to help himself to whiskey.

Fill up glass with sweet cider

STONE WALL

Use large bar glass, with 3 or 4 lumps of ice.

1 teaspoon sugar.
1 jigger of whiskey.
1 bottle of plain soda.

Stir well, remove ice and serve.

ST. CHARLES PUNCH

Use large bar glass.

1 teaspoon sugar.
3 dashes of lemon juice.
1 dash seltzer.
1 jigger port wine.
½ jigger brandy.
2 dashes Curaçao.
1 dash Dr. Siegert's Genuine Angostura Bitters.

Stir well, fill glass with shaved ice, trim with fruit and serve with straws.

ST. CROIX CRUSTA

Use mixing glass half full of ice.

3 dashes of gum syrup.
1 dash of Peychaud Bitters.
3 dashes Dr. Siegert's Genuine Angostura Bitters.
2 dashes of lemon juice.
1 dash of mineral water.
2 dashes Maraschino.
1 jigger St. Croix rum.

Mix well, strain into stem glass, prepared as follows: Remove the peel from one lemon in one long string, put into stem glass after moistening and dipping in sugar.

ST. CROIX FIX

Large bar glass half full of ice.

2 teaspoons sugar.
3 dashes of lemon juice.
3 dashes of pineapple syrup.
1 dash of seltzer.
1 jigger of St. Croix rum.

Recipes for Mixing Fancy Drinks

1 dash Dr. Siegert's Genuine Angostura Bitters.

Stir well, fill up with ice, trim with fruit, serve with straw.

ST. CROIX RUM PUNCH

Use large bar glass half full of ice.

1 tablespoon sugar.
3 or 4 dashes of lemon juice.
1 dash of mineral water.
1 dash of Jamaica rum.
1 dash Dr. Siegert's Genuine Angostura Bitters.
1 jigger of St. Croix rum.
1 slice of lemon.

Stir well, fill up with ice, trim with fruit, serve with straw.

ST. CROIX RUM FIZZ

Use large bar glass half full of ice.

½ tablespoon sugar.
3 or 4 dashes of lemon juice.
White of 1 egg.
1 jigger of St. Croix rum.

Shake well, strain into fizz glass, fill up with seltzer or carbonated water and serve.

ST. CROIX SOUR

Use large bar glass half full of ice.

½ tablespoon sugar.
1 dash mineral water.
1 jigger St. Croix rum.

Shake well, strain into sour glass with slice of lemon and serve.

TANSY AND WHISKEY

Put Tansy Sprigs into a quart bottle and fill up with liquor of any kind. A bottle filled in this manner with tansy should last

50

through a season, as bottle can be refilled with liquor as long as strength lasts.

TIP TOP PUNCH

Use large bar glass, with 5 lumps of ice.
1 dash of lemon juice.
1 lump of loaf sugar.
2 slices of pineapple.
1 slice of orange.

Fill up with champagne, stir well, dress with berries, dash with Dr. Siegert's Genuine Angostura Bitters, serve with straw.

TOM AND JERRY

Use large bowl.

Take the whites of any number of eggs and beat to a stiff froth.

Add 1 ½ tablespoons of powdered sugar to each egg.

Beat the yolks of the eggs separate.

Stir well together and beat till you have a stiff batter. Add to this as much bicarbonate of soda as will cover a nickel. Stir up frequently, so that eggs will not separate or settle.

(To serve.)

Put 1 tablespoonful of batter into Tom and Jerry mug.

1 jigger rum and brandy mixed.

Fill up with boiling water or milk; grate nutmeg on top; stir with spoon and serve.

TOM COLLINS GIN

Use large bar glass with 3 or 4 lumps of ice.
1 tablespoon sugar.
3 or 4 dashes of lemon juice.
1 jigger Old Tom Gin.
1 bottle plain soda.

Stir with spoon; take out ice, and serve.

Recipes for Mixing Fancy Drinks

TOM COLLINS BRANDY

Mix same as above, substituting brandy in place of gin.

TOM COLLINS WHISKEY

Mix same as above, substituting whiskey for brandy.

TOM COLLINS RUM

Mix same as above, substitute rum in place of whiskey.

TRILBY COCKTAIL

Use mixing glass half full of ice.
2 dashes of orange bitters.
2 dashes Dr. Siegert's Genuine Angostura Bitters.
½ jigger Tom Gin.
½ jigger vermouth (Italian).
Stir well; strain into cocktail glass; add cherry, and float creme d'yvette on top.

TURF COCKTAIL

Use mixing glass ½ full of ice.
2 dashes Absinthe.
2 dashes Maraschino.
2 dashes Orange Bitters.
1 dash Dr. Siegert's Genuine Angostura Bitters.
½ jigger French vermouth.
½ jigger Plymouth Gin.
Stir well; strain in cocktail glass; put in olive, and serve.

TURKISH SHERBET

Use a punch bowl.
Mix as follows:
2 quarts of sweet wine.
2 quarts of water.

4 pounds of sugar.
½ wine glass of Dr. Siegert's Genuine Angostura Bitters.
4 lemons, juice only.
6 oranges, juice only.
1 pound blanched almonds.
1 pound muscatel grapes.
½ pound figs, cut up.
½ pound seedless raisins.
1⅓ dozen eggs, whites only.
1 dozen cloves, a small piece of cinnamon and a little caramel coloring.

Make a hot syrup of the sugar and water and pour it over the raisins, cloves and cinnamon.

When cool, add orange and lemon juice and wine. Strain and freeze in the usual manner.

Take out the spices and add the scalded raisins, figs, grapes and almonds last.

TUXEDO COCKTAIL

Use mixing glass half full of ice.

1 dash Maraschino.
1 dash of Absinthe.
3 dashes Dr. Siegert's Genuine Angostura Bitters.
½ jigger French vermouth.
½ Old Tom Gin.

Stir well; strain in cocktail glass; add cherry, and serve.

VANILLA PUNCH

Use large bar glass.

1 tablespoon of sugar, dissolved in water.
2 dashes curaçao.
3 dashes lemon juice.
1 dash Dr. Siegert's Genuine Angostura Bitters.
½ jigger vanilla cordial.
1 jigger of cognac brandy.

Stir well; fill up with ice; trim with fruit; serve with straws.

Recipes for Mixing Fancy Drinks

VERMOUTH COCKTAIL

Use mixing glass ½ full of ice.
3 dashes gum syrup.
4 dashes Dr. Siegert's Genuine Angostura Bitters.
1 jigger Vermouth.
Stir well; strain into cocktail glass; add fruit, and serve.

VIRGIN COCKTAIL

Use mixing glass ½ full of ice.
3 dashes Dr. Siegert's Genuine Angostura Bitters.
2 dashes raspberry syrup.
½ jigger vermouth.
½ jigger Plymouth Gin.
Stir well; strain in cocktail glass, and serve.

WHISKEY COBBLER

Use large bar glass.
½ tablespoon sugar dissolved in water.
1 dash maraschino.
1 dash Dr. Siegert's Genuine Angostura Bitters.
1 jigger of whiskey.
1 slice of orange, quartered.
Fill up with ice; stir well; dress with fruits, and serve with straws.

WHISKEY COCKTAIL

Use mixing glass ½ full of ice.
2 dashes Dr. Siegert's Genuine Angostura Bitters.
2 dashes syrup.
2 dashes orange bitters or curaçao.
1 jigger whiskey.
Stir well; twist lemon peel on top, and serve. In making cocktails of any kind, if customer desires them dry omit the syrup.

WHISKEY CRUSTA

Prepare this drink same as Brandy Crusta, using whiskey for brandy.

WHISKEY DAISY

Prepare this drink same as Brandy Daisy, substituting whiskey for brandy.

WHISKEY FIX

Prepare this drink same as Brandy or Gin Fix, substituting whiskey for other liquors.

WHISKEY FIZZ

Prepare this drink same as a Gin Fizz, substituting whiskey for gin.

WHISKEY FLIP

Prepare this drink same as Gin Flip, substituting whiskey for gin.

WHISKEY PUNCH

Use large bar glass half full of ice.
1 teaspoon sugar.
4 or 5 dashes lemon juice.
1 jigger whiskey and rum mixed.
1 dash Dr. Siegert's Genuine Angostura Bitters.

Shake well; strain into punch glass, with slice of orange; 3 or 4 dashes of Curaçao on top, with seltzer, and serve.

WHISKEY RICKEY

Prepare this drink as Gin Rickey, using whiskey instead of gin.

WHISKEY SOUR

Use large bar glass, half full ice.
1 teaspoon sugar.

Recipes for Mixing Fancy Drinks

4 or 5 dashes lemon juice.

1 jigger whiskey.

Shake well; strain into sour glass; add pineapple and dash with seltzer, and serve.

WHISKEY TODDY

1 teaspoonful sugar.

1 teaspoonful water.

1 jigger of whiskey.

Dissolve sugar in a little water; add the whiskey; stir with a spoon, and serve.

WHITE LION

Use large bar glass, half full of ice.

1 teaspoon pulverized sugar.

Juice of ½ lime or lemon.

1 jigger of Santa Cruz rum.

3 dashes curaçao.

3 dashes raspberry.

Shake well; strain into a stem glass, and serve.

WHITE PLUSH

Use whiskey glass.

Allow customer to help himself to bourbon or rye whiskey, then fill glass with milk.

WIDOW'S DREAM COCKTAIL

Use cocktail glass.

1 jigger benedictine.

1 fresh egg.

Fill up with milk and cream, and serve.

Special Drinks for the Soda Fountain and Other Recipes

ANCIENT BITTERS

½ glass shaved ice.
4 dashes Dr. Siegert's Genuine Angostura Bitters.
2 dashes elixir calisaya.
4 dashes Curaçao Cordial.
2 dashes compound tincture gentian.
1 ounce cherry malt phosphate syrup.

Shake well and add enough soda to fill 8-ounce glass. Serve in mineral water glass.

ANGOSTURA GINGER ALE

1 glass ginger ale.
3 dashes Dr. Siegert's Genuine Angostura Bitters.

ANGOSTURA EGG PHOSPHATE

An egg phosphate.
Add 1 teaspoon Dr. Siegert's Genuine Angostura Bitters.

ANGOSTURA FIZZ

Bar glass.
Tablespoon powdered sugar.
Juice half a lemon.
Broken ice.
Pony Dr. Siegert's Genuine Angostura Bitters.
White of an egg.
Tablespoon of cream.
Seltzer.

Shake well in shaker.

ANGOSTURA GRAPE FRUIT

Cut the fruit in half, extract the core or pithy substance in the center with a sharp knife; insert the knife around the inner edge of the peel and disengage the fruit

Soda Fountain Drinks

from the peel without removing the fruit or
breaking the peel; sprinkle plentifully with
powdered sugar and dash the opening caused
by the removal of the core with Dr. Siegert's
Genuine Angostura Bitters.   Ice well before
serving.

ANGOSTURA PHOSPHATE

Use a phosphate glass.

½ teaspoonful acid phosphate.

1 teaspoonful Dr. Siegert's Angostura
Bitters.   (THE ONLY GENUINE.)

2 tablespoonfuls lemon syrup, or juice of ½
lemon well sweetened.

Fill glass with carbonic water.

ANGOSTURA SHERBET

This delightful and popular sherbet is made
by adding about ½ wine glass of Dr. Siegert's
Genuine Angostura Bitters to each pint of
lemon ice.

BANCROFT PUNCH

¾ ounce vanilla syrup.

1 egg.

½ ounce sweet cream.

¾ ounce brandy.

6 dashes Dr. Siegert's Genuine Angostura
Bitters.

Shake till egg is well beaten; put in mug;
fill with hot milk; top with whipped cream
and grated nutmeg.

BICYCLE COCKTAIL

½ glass ginger ale.

½ glass milk.

1 teaspoon Dr. Siegert's Genuine Angostura
Bitters.

" BOXER " FLIPPE

Mixing glass half full shaved ice.
4 dashes Dr. Siegert's Genuine Angostura
Bitters.
2 oz. port wine.
½ oz. ginger ale syrup.
1 oz. lemon syrup.
Add soda from large stream.
Pour from shaker to tumbler several times
and serve with slice of pineapple or orange.

BROADWAY FLIP

Put in mixing glass two large sprays of
mint.
1 ½ oz. blood orange syrup.
2 dashes acid phosphate.
1 egg.
Fill glass half full shaved ice, shake well
and strain. Add fine stream soda, toss several
times, grate nutmeg on top and serve with
straws.

CARDINAL PUNCH

Make a syrup of two pounds of sugar and
one quart of water; to this add the rind of
two oranges and the juice of four, one ounce
of whole cloves and one stick of whole cinnamon. Then add two quarts of red wine, half
pint of port wine and one gill of Cognac; 1
wine glass Dr. Siegert's Genuine Angostura
Bitters; strain and freeze. When half frozen,
add one pint of wine jelly, then continue
freezing until done.

CHERRY SANGAREE

1 ounce cherry syrup.
½ ounce sherry wine.
2 dashes Dr. Siegert's Genuine Angostura
Bitters.
2 teaspoons powdered sugar.
1 slice lemon, 1 slice orange.

Soda Fountain Drinks

Draw coarse stream, stir and serve with straws. Use 12 oz. bell glass. Slice of lemon and orange to be added when drink is finished.

CHERRY MAZE

(8 oz. mineral.)

1 oz. cherry syrup.
1 dash Dr. Siegert's Genuine Angostura Bitters.
⅔ ice; soda; strain and add one cherry.

CIDER COCKTAIL

(Cocktail Glass.)

½ ice.
4 drams sugar.
2 dashes Dr. Siegert's Genuine Angostura Bitters.
4 ounces cider.
Mix and strain; twist slice lemon on top.

CLARET COCKTAIL

1 ounce of claret.
2 ounces of simple syrup.
2 dashes of lemon juice.
1 dash Dr. Siegert's Genuine Angostura Bitters.
Lemonade glass half full of cracked ice, pour all together, stir well, then fill glass with soda, strain into a 6 ounce glass, twist a small piece of lemon rind and add cherries.

CLARET RINGUE

1 ounce claret syrup.
1 ounce lemon syrup.

½ ounce port wine.
1 dash Dr. Siegert's Genuine Angostura Bitters.
½ ounce sweet cream.
Mix and serve in 5 ounce glass.

EGG PHOSPHATE

Use large bar glass ½ full fine ice.

1 teaspoon sugar.
1 teaspoon of acid phosphate.
1 whole egg.
Fill glass with water; shake well; strain into lemonade glass, and serve.

For Angostura Egg Phosphate add one teaspoon Angostura Bitters.

EGG TODDY

1 egg.
1 ounce Malt Extract.
1 ounce grape syrup.
3 dashes Dr. Siegert's Genuine Angostura Bitters.
A little ice.
Proceed as in Phosphate.

ELK'S DELIGHT

Juice of ½ orange.
Juice of ½ lemon.
1 ounce pure grape juice.
2 teaspoonfuls powdered sugar.
1 dash Dr. Siegert's Genuine Angostura Bitters.
Cracked ice to half fill glass, plain water to finish; shake, serve in 12 ounce lemonade glass. Garnish with slice of orange and cherry.

EUREKA BISQUE

Mixing glass ½ full of cracked ice.
½ ounce brandy.
1 egg.
1 ounce plain syrup.
1 dash Dr. Siegert's Genuine Angostura Bitters.
Shake, add enough ginger ale to fill glass when strained into a 12 ounce bell glass. Shake cinnamon on the top.

61

Soda Fountain Drinks

FLINCH FRAPPE

¾ ounce strawberry syrup.
¾ ounce pineapple syrup.
1 ounce sweet cream.
1 dash Dr. Siegert's Genuine Angostura Bitters.

Small quantity of ice cream, shake well, put in 12 ounce glass, add a little soda, small stream, and ice cream to fill up glass. Garnish with pineapple and cherry.

GINGER ALE COBBLER

1 ½ ounce ginger ale syrup.
½ ounce orange syrup.
½ glass shaved ice.
1 dash Dr. Siegert's Genuine Angostura Bitters.
Slice of pineapple.

Fill glass with plain soda and stir with spoon.

GRAPE FRUIT COBBLER

Juice of one-half lemon or lime.
2 ounces of Kitro syrup.

Fill glass nearly full cracked ice, 2 dashes Dr. Siegert's Genuine Angostura Bitters, ½ ounce sherry wine, shake, pour in fancy cobbler glass and dress with slice of orange.

GRAPE ICE

2 pounds of sugar.
2 lemons.
1 orange.
2 quarts of red Tokay grapes.
1 tablespoon Dr. Siegert's Genuine Angostura Bitters.
1 quart water.

Put grapes, sugar and water in a kettle and place over a slow fire, under constant stirring bring it to a boil, then pass it through a sieve, leaving skins and pits behind. Squeeze the lemons and orange and add the juice. When cold freeze in the usual manner. If this is to be served in glasses, beat up four egg whites quite stiff and mix it into the batch smooth and foamy. A few drops of red color should be added, to give it a more positive appearance, and two or three whole grapes placed on each portion.

JERSEY CREAM PUFF

Take an empty cream puff, cut off the top with a pair of shears, then fill the cream puff two-thirds full of ice cream; put on a ladle of crushed fruit, half a ladle of whipped cream, and on the top place a creme d'yvette cherry. Take the top you have cut off and place it about half over the top and serve. Creme d'yvette cherries are not on the market, so take a bottle of maraschino cherries (white), pour off the maraschino, and pour over creme d'yvette. (Marie Brizard brand is the most effective.) Creme de Menthe cherries may be made the same way and are very delicious.

KOLA COOLER

½ ounce kola punch.

½ ounce red cherry syrup.

½ ounce pineapple syrup.

2 dashes Dr. Siegert's Genuine Angostura Bitters.

Serve in 12 ounce soda, two-thirds full cracked ice, with straws.

LEMON EGGNOG

1 ounce lemon syrup.

1 egg.

2 dashes Dr. Siegert's Genuine Angostura Bitters.

63

Soda Fountain Drinks

1 dram rum wine.
Cracked ice.
Shake well, add soda from fine stream.
Strain and serve like Egg Phosphate.

LEMON ICE

4 quarts of water.
10 lemons.
4 ½ pounds of sugar.

Grate half the lemons as described in the foregoing formulas, squeeze out, and put rind, juice, half the water and the sugar into a pan, set it on the fire and stir until the sugar is dissolved and it becomes quite warm. Then remove and add the remaining two quarts of water and strain into the freezer. Freeze in the usual manner. Some makers add a few egg whites before freezing or when half frozen: this is not recommended, as it makes the ice too light and the consequence is that the ice will become icy and rough after standing any length of time. One wine glass of Dr. Siegert's Genuine Angostura Bitters added to the above before freezing lends a delightful flavor.

LEMON SHERBET

2 pints lemon juice from nice fresh juicy lemons.
4 pints simple syrup.
6 pints water.
White of 1 egg well beaten.

Mix and freeze.

MANHATTAN FIZZ

1 ½ ounce lemon syrup.
1 tablespoon ice cream.

4 dashes rum.
1 dash Dr. Siegert's Genuine Angostura
Bitters.
Shake and draw fine soda stream; serve in
large glasses; sprinkle cinnamon on top.

MELON SUNDAE

Take a small-sized cantaloupe, cut in two,
remove the seeds, slice off a small portion
from the bottom so that it may stand square-
ly. Place in the half of the cantaloupe the
usual amount of ice cream. Top with crushed
pineapple and whole cherries. Insert spoon
upright in meat of cantaloupe. Place upon
napkin and serve on fancy plate.

MIDNIGHT ON THE MIDWAY

1 ounce claret syrup.
½ ounce Kola syrup.
1 dash lemon juice.
1 dash Dr. Siegert's Genuine Angostura
Bitters.
⅔ ice.
Fill with ginger ale, etc.

MILK AND MINT

8-ounce glass.
1 ounce mint syrup.
½ dram Dr. Siegert's Genuine Angostura
Bitters.
2 ounces milk.
Soda, q. s.

MORNING GLORY

1 teaspoon sugar.
1 raw egg.
Shaved ice.
Fill glass with milk.
1 teaspoon Dr. Siegert's Genuine Angostura
Bitters on top.
Shake well before adding Angostura.

Soda Fountain Drinks

ORANGE ICE

The same formula is observed as for Lemon Ice, except that you use six oranges and two lemons, grating the rind of two oranges, adding it to the batch before it is heated.

ORANGE SHERBET

3 quarts of water.
8 pounds of icing sugar.
Cook the above to a boil, set off and add the juice of 3 dozen oranges, the gratings of two orange peels, juice of 1 dozen lemons and the whites of 6 eggs.

OXFORD CORDIAL

Another individual name for a special beverage which is seldom made alike in different places. Generally it is served as a phosphate with lemon and raspberry syrup and a dash of Jamaica rum, with 4 dashes Dr. Siegert's Genuine Angostura Bitters.

PICK-ME-UP OR DAY DAWN

1 ounce vanilla syrup.
30 grains Pot. Brom.
3 dashes Dr. Siegert's Genuine Angostura Bitters.
½ ice.
Fill with milk and shake.

PING PONG PUNCH

(1) 1 ounce orange syrup.
½ ounce lemon syrup.
1 ounce claret wine.
½ ounce grape juice.
3 dashes Dr. Siegert's Genuine Angostura Bitters.
1 egg, a little cracked ice, shake, then fill

with soda as in other egg drinks, strain and
serve.

(2) 1 ½ ounce orange syrup.
½ ounce claret wine.
1 ounce grape juice.
3 dashes Dr. Siegert's Genuine Angostura
Bitters.
1 egg, ¼ glass cracked ice, shake, strain,
toss and serve.

RASPBERRY ROYAL

Place 1 ounce raspberry syrup (double
strength) in a 6 ounce cup; add a dash of
phosphate and fill with hot water. Sprinkle
with grated nutmeg, and top with whipped
cream.

ROYAL FLIP

¾ ounce strawberry syrup.
¾ ounce pineapple syrup.
1 egg.
2 ounces sweet cream.
4 dashes Dr. Siegert's Genuine Angostura
Bitters.
Small quantity shaved ice.

Shake, strain, use full stream soda; pour
from glass to shaker a time or two; grate
nutmeg on top.

SIBERIAN FLIP

1 ounce orange syrup.
1 ounce pineapple syrup.
1 dash Dr. Siegert's Genuine Angostura
Bitters.
2 dashes Phos.
Soda, etc.

SOUTHERN SHERBET

1 ounce claret syrup.
1 ounce pineapple syrup.
¼ ounce lime juice.
2 dashes Dr. Siegert's Geruine Angostura
Bitters.
Serve in eight ounce mineral with cracked
ice and top off with Sundae pineapple.

Soda Fountain Drinks

SUMMER PUNCH

Steep two generous teaspoonfuls of tea in two quarts of boiling water for five minutes. Then strain and add one pound of lump sugar, stirring until thoroughly dissolved. Grate the peel of eight good-sized lemons and extract all the juice. Cut three oranges into slices, shred one pineapple, slice five bananas very thin and hull one pint of strawberries. When the tea is cold, add all the fruit, dash with Dr. Siegert's Genuine Angostura Bitters and let stand in the refrigerator for several hours. Place a cube of ice in the punch bowl, pour the mixture around it, and when well chilled serve in punch glasses. To get the best results from the pineapple, peel and remove the eyes, tear apart with a silver fork, reject the cores, sprinkle with sugar and let stand on the ice for twelve hours.

TOKAY PUNCH

Out of six pounds of tokay grapes, select one pound to be put into the punch last. Now make a boiling syrup of three pounds of sugar and one quart of water and pour this over the remaining five pounds of grapes. When partly cold, rub it through a sieve, leaving skins and seeds behind, then add the juice of two oranges and two lemons and one quart of St. Julien claret, a half wine glass of Dr. Siegert's Genuine Angostura Bitters, then strain and freeze. Before serving add one pint of good brandy and an Italian meringue paste of six egg whites, colored a nice red, and drop in the remaining grapes.

TONIQUE FIZZ

Fill glass half full shaved ice, add white of one egg, three spoons powdered sugar, three dashes Dr. Siegert's Genuine Angostura Bitters, four dashes lime juice, eight dashes phosphate. Shake well, pour into twelve-ounce bell top glass and fill with vichy in short dashes to make fizz.

TUTTI-FRUTTI ICE

Take one pint of simple syrup, one pint of water, one gill of kirschwasser, a teaspoonful of pure vanilla extract, two teaspoonfuls Dr. Siegert's Genuine Angostura Bitters, the juice of two lemons and a pint of mixed fruits, cut into small pieces; mix the syrup, water, liquor, vanilla and lemon juice, and freeze the mixture; then mix into it a meringue mass, made of the whites of two eggs and two ounces of powdered sugar, freeze again and then add the fruit; mix them ligh.ly but thoroughly well in; the ice may then be molded and buried in ice and salt till needed for use.

TUTTI-FRUTTI PUNCH

Combinations of fruit flavors may be varied indefinitely. The special character-istic of the following recipe is found in the Maraschino cherries, which give a peculiar zest to the whole. Boil together for five min-utes one quart of water and one pound of sugar. Add the grated rinds of two lemons and four oranges and continue boiling for ten minutes longer. Strain the syrup through cheese cloth and add one quart of cold water. Extract the juice from the lemons and oranges,

Soda Fountain Drinks

strain and mix with two dozen Malaga grapes
cut in half and seeded, two sliced Tangerine
oranges, four slices of pineapple, one banana
cut in slices, and one pint bottle of Maraschino cherries, with their liquor, the cherries
being halved, two teaspoons Dr. Siegert's
Genuine Angostura Bitters. Serve from a
punch bowl in which a cube of ice has been
placed.

VIRGINIA JULEP

¼ ounce Creme de Menthe syrup.
½ ounce lemon syrup.
3 dashes port wine.
1 dash Dr. Siegert's Genuine Angostura
Bitters.
2 Sundae cherries.
Serve in 8-ounce mineral. Add sprig fresh
mint.

WESTERN WINNER

½ ounce red raspberry syrup.
½ ounce lemon syrup.
1 ounce orange syrup.
1 dash Dr. Siegert's Genuine Angostura
Bitters.
Serve in 12-ounce soda, two-thirds glass
cracked ice, with straw.

YALE SLING

½ ounce raspberry syrup.
1 ¼ ounce grape syrup.
½ ounce Catawba wine.
1 dash Dr. Siegert's Genuine Angostura
Bitters.
Serve in 8-ounce mineral with cracked ice.

CLARET AND ANGOSTURA

To add body to ordinary table claret and give it a rich Burgundy flavor, add one tablespoon Dr. Siegert's Genuine Angostura Bitters to every quart of claret. By using this proportion of Bitters in claret cup, a much smaller quantity of claret is required, and the flavor of the cup is greatly improved.

------◄◆►------

ATTRACTIVE DESSERTS

ANGOSTURA CAKE ICING

A delightful icing is made by adding a tablespoon of Angostura Bitters to each pint of icing.

ANGOSTURA LEMON JELLY

1 box of Knox's Sparkling Gelatine.
1 cup of cold water.
3 cups of boiling water.
1 ½ cups of sugar.
1 pint of lemon juice.
1 ½ tablespoons Dr. Siegert's Genuine Angostura Bitters.

Soak the gelatine in the cold water five minutes and dissolve with the boiling water; add the sugar and stir until dissolved and cooled; then add the lemon juice and Angostura and strain through a cheese cloth into molds.

ANGOSTURA ORANGE JELLY

½ a box of Knox's Sparkling Gelatine.
1 cup of sugar.
½ a cup of cold water.
Juice of one lemon.
1 cup of boiling water.
1 pint of orange juice.
1 tablespoon Dr. Siegert's Genuine Angostura Bitters.

Attractive Desserts

Remove the juice from the oranges with a spoon, to avoid the oil in the rind. Prepare as Angostura lemon jelly, but strain the liquid before the adding of the orange juice, that the little particles of orange pulp may be retained.

ANGOSTURA WINE JELLY

½ a box of Knox's Sparkling Gelatine.
1 cup of sugar.
½ a cup of cold water.
1 cup of wine.
2 cups of boiling water.
Juice of two lemons.
1 tablespoon Dr. Siegert's Genuine Angostura Bitters.

Proceed as in Angostura lemon jelly; add the wine and fruit juice when the dissolving sugar has cooled the liquid.

ANGOSTURA GRAPE-FRUIT JELLY

½ a box of Knox's Sparkling Gelatine.
½ cup of cold water.
1 cup of boiling water.
1 cup or less of sugar.
Juice of one lemon.
½ a cup of sherry wine.
2 cups of grape fruit juice and pulp.
1 tablespoon Dr. Siegert's Genuine Angostura Bitters.

Prepare with Knox's Sparkling Gelatine according to directions previously given. Add the grape-fruit juice and pulp and the sherry and Angostura after the liquid has been strained and become cool. Do not pour into the molds set in ice water until the jelly is just ready to set, in order to avoid settling of the pulp.

FRUIT MOLDED IN ANGOSTURA JELLY

Make an Angostura lemon, orange or wine jelly with Knox's Sparkling Gelatine according to previous directions. Set a plain mold in broken ice and water, and dip thin slices of fruit or almonds and pistachios in liquid jelly and arrange on the bottom and sides of the mold according to some design. Carefully add a spoonful or two of jelly to hold the nuts or fruit in place, then, alternately, fruit and jelly to fill the mold. Sliced bananas, white grapes skinned and seeded, candied cherries, figs cut in shreds, and orange sections from which the membrane has been removed, either singly or in combination, are good. Serve with whipped cream or thin custard.

FANCY ANGOSTURA JELLY

Make an Angostura lemon or wine jelly; dissolve and color such portion of a package of Knox's Sparkling Gelatine as is desired in a tablespoonful of water and add to it one-half the liquid jelly. Pour this into a mold, and when set pour in the untinted part of the jelly, or mold in separate molds and cut into cubes to use as garnish in carrying out a pink "color scheme."

ANGOSTURA MAY WINE PUNCH

Use a large punch bowl.

Take one or two bunches of fresh mint or Woodruff, and cut it up in two or three lengths, place it into a large bar glass, and fill up the balance with French brandy, cover it up and let it stand for two or three hours, until the essence of the Woodruff is thoroughly extracted; cover the bottom of the bowl with loaf sugar, and pour from 4 to 6 bottles of plain soda water over the sugar.

Cut up 6 oranges in slices.

½ pineapple, and sufficient berries and grapes.

8 bottles of Rhine or Moselle wine.

1 bottle of champagne

Attractive Desserts

6 tablespoons Dr. Siegert's Genuine Angostura Bitters.

Then put mint or Woodruff and brandy, etc., into bowl, and stir with the ladle.

Surround the bowl with ice, serve in a wine glass in such a manner that each customer will get a piece of all the fruits contained in the punch.

See that your dealer gives you Dr. Siegert's, the only genuine Angostura Bitters.

ANGOSTURA GRAPE FRUIT

Cut the fruit in half, extract the core or pithy substance in the center with a sharp knife; insert the knife around the inner edge of the peel and disengage the fruit from the peel without removing the fruit or breaking the peel; sprinkle plentifully with powdered sugar and dash the opening caused by the removal of the core with equal parts of sherry and Dr. Siegert's Genuine Angostura Bitters. Ice well before serving.

Your friend will recognize you as a connoisseur if you offer him Angostura with his sherry.

ANGOSTURA SHERBET

This delightful and popular sherbet is made by adding about ½ wine glass of Dr. Siegert's Genuine Angostura Bitters to each pint of lemon ice.

GRAPE ICE

2 pounds of sugar.
2 quarts of red Tokay grapes.
2 lemons.

1 tablespoon Dr. Siegert's Genuine Angostura Bitters.

1 orange.

1 quart water.

Put grapes, sugar and water in a kettle and place over a slow fire, under constant stirring bring it to a boil, then pass it through a sieve, leaving skins and pits behind. Squeeze the lemons and orange and add the juice. When cold, freeze in the usual manner. If this is to be served in glasses, beat up four egg whites quite stiff and mix it into the batch smooth and foamy.

" The man who knows " always adds Angostura to his drink — it's a great tonic flavoring.

YEARLY CALENDAR, 1909

JANUARY

S	M	T	W	T	F	S
.	.	.	.	.	1	2
3	4	5	6	7	8	9
10	11	12	13	14	15	16
17	18	19	20	21	22	23
24	25	26	27	28	29	30
31	.	.	.	.	.	.

JULY

S	M	T	W	T	F	S
.	.	.	.	1	2	3
4	5	6	7	8	9	10
11	12	13	14	15	16	17
18	19	20	21	22	23	24
25	26	27	28	29	30	31

FEBRUARY

S	M	T	W	T	F	S
.	1	2	3	4	5	6
7	8	9	10	11	12	13
14	15	16	17	18	19	20
21	22	23	24	25	26	27
28	.	.	.	.	.	.

AUGUST

S	M	T	W	T	F	S
1	2	3	4	5	6	7
8	9	10	11	12	13	14
15	16	17	18	19	20	21
22	23	24	25	26	27	28
29	30	31	.	.	.	.

MARCH

S	M	T	W	T	F	S
.	1	2	3	4	5	6
7	8	9	10	11	12	13
14	15	16	17	18	19	20
21	22	23	24	25	26	27
28	29	30	31	.	.	.

SEPTEMBER

S	M	T	W	T	F	S
.	.	.	1	2	3	4
5	6	7	8	9	10	11
12	13	14	15	16	17	18
19	20	21	22	23	24	25
26	27	28	29	30	.	.

APRIL

S	M	T	W	T	F	S
.	.	.	.	1	2	3
4	5	6	7	8	9	10
11	12	13	14	15	16	17
18	19	20	21	22	23	24
25	26	27	28	29	30	.

OCTOBER

S	M	T	W	T	F	S
.	.	.	.	.	1	2
3	4	5	6	7	8	9
10	11	12	13	14	15	16
17	18	19	20	21	22	23
24	25	26	27	28	29	30
31	.	.	.	.	.	.

MAY

S	M	T	W	T	F	S
.	.	.	.	.	.	1
2	3	4	5	6	7	8
9	10	11	12	13	14	15
16	17	18	19	20	21	22
23	24	25	26	27	28	29
30	31	.	.	.	.	.

NOVEMBER

S	M	T	W	T	F	S
.	1	2	3	4	5	6
7	8	9	10	11	12	13
14	15	16	17	18	19	20
21	22	23	24	25	26	27
28	29	30	.	.	.	.

JUNE

S	M	T	W	T	F	S
.	.	1	2	3	4	5
6	7	8	9	10	11	12
13	14	15	16	17	18	19
20	21	22	23	24	25	26
27	28	29	30	.	.	.

DECEMBER

S	M	T	W	T	F	S
.	.	.	1	2	3	4
5	6	7	8	9	10	11
12	13	14	15	16	17	18
19	20	21	22	23	24	25
26	27	28	29	30	31	.